# Peppy Penguins

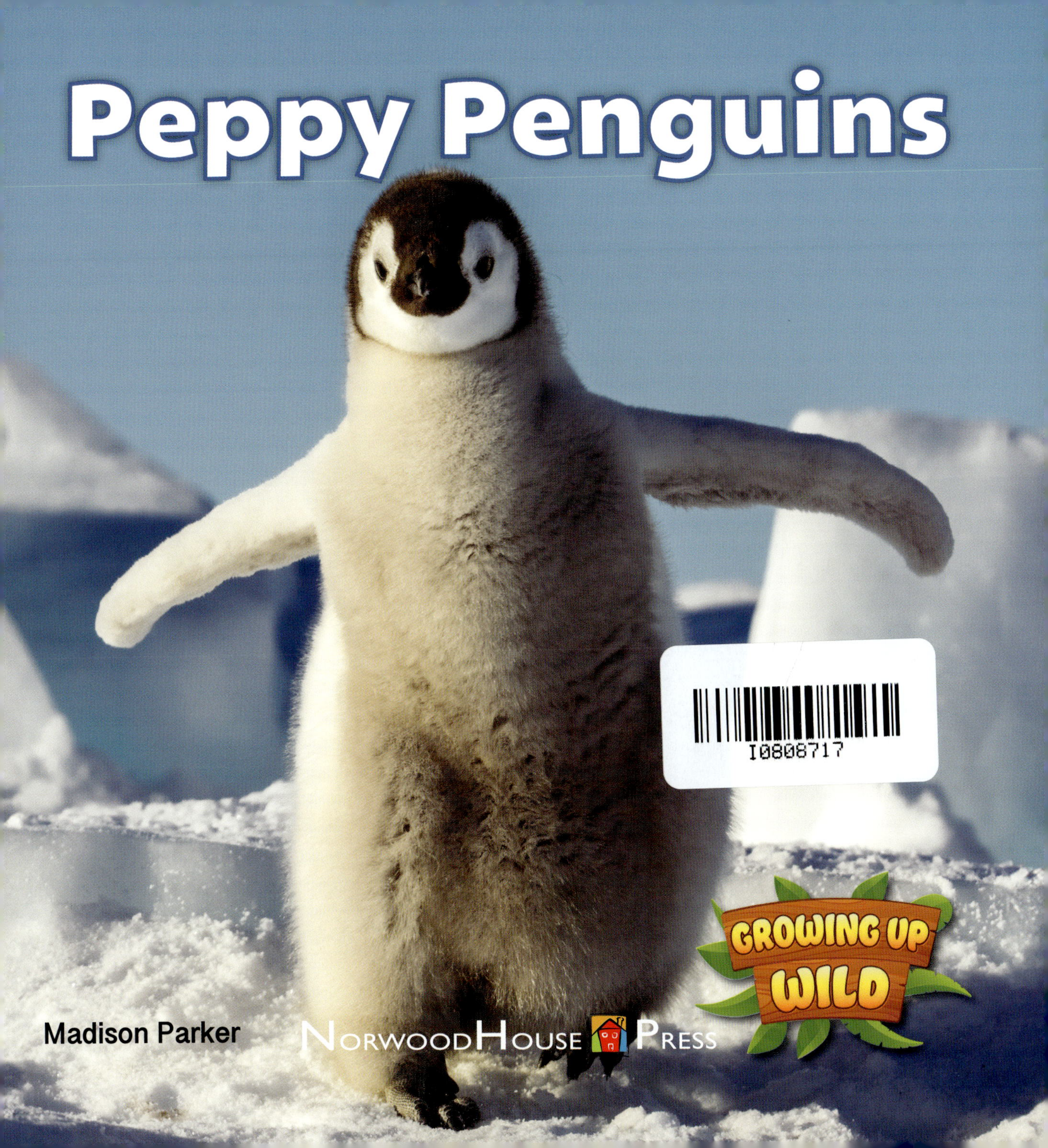



Growing Up Wild

Madison Parker

Norwood House Press

**Cataloging-in-Publication Data**

Names: Parker, Madison.
Title: Peppy penguins / Madison Parker.
Description: Buffalo, NY : Norwood House Press, 2026. | Series: Growing up wild | Includes glossary and index.
Identifiers: ISBN 9781978574144 (pbk.) | ISBN 9781978574151 (library bound) | ISBN 9781978574168 (ebook)
Subjects: LCSH: Penguins--Infancy--Juvenile literature. | Penguins--Juvenile literature.
Classification: LCC QL696.S473 P375 2026 | DDC 598.4713'92--dc23

Published in 2026 by
**Norwood House Press**
2544 Clinton Street
Buffalo, NY 14224


Designer: Rhea Magaro
Editor: Kim Thompson

Photo credits: Cover, p. 1 Risto Raunio/Shutterstock.com; pp. 5, 17, 21 Vladsilver /Shutterstock.com; p. 6 MagicBloods /Shutterstock.com; pp. 8, 9 Drop Zone Drone / Shutterstock.com; p. 10 Nick Dale Photo /Shutterstock.com; p. 11 Pav-Pro Photography Ltd /Shutterstock.com; p. 13 NicoELNino /Shutterstock.com; p. 14 LovieLea / Shutterstock.com ;p. 15 Patrick Poendl /Shutterstock.com; p. 18 Hanneke Wetzer /Shutterstock.com;p. 19 Uswatun des /Shutterstock.com;



Printed in the United States of America



CPSIA compliance information: Batch #CSNHP26: For further information contact Norwood House Press at 1-800-237-9932.

# TABLE OF CONTENTS

# Peppy Penguins

Penguins grow up in the **wild**.

Baby penguins are called chicks.

## How Baby Penguins Look

Baby penguins are covered with **down**.

The down can be brown, black, or gray.

Baby penguins have beaks. They have **webbed** feet.

They have wings, but they cannot fly.

# How Baby Penguins Sound

Baby penguins make sounds to **communicate**. They call to their parents.

When chicks and parents find each other, they make happy chirps.

# What Baby Penguins Eat

Baby penguins are **carnivores**.

They eat meat from ocean animals.

Penguin parents catch fish, **krill**, or squid.

Parents **regurgitate** the food into the baby's mouth.

## Lots to Learn

A group of penguins is called a **colony**. Chicks stay with their colony. This protects them from danger.

Baby penguins wait months for their feathers to grow in. Their new feathers are **waterproof**.

Chicks with feathers can learn to swim. They can learn to dive for fish.

## All Grown Up

Young penguins with feathers are **mature**. They leave their parents. They swim out to sea.

# Glossary

**carnivores** (KAHR-nuh-vorz): animals that eat only meat

**colony** (KAH-luh-nee): a group of animals of the same kind living together

**communicate** (kuh-MYOO-ni-kate): to share information and feelings

**down** (doun): the soft, fluffy, non-waterproof feathers that cover baby penguins

**krill** (krill): small, shrimp-like creatures that live in the ocean

**mature** (muh-CHOOR): fully grown or developed; adult

**regurgitate** (ri-GUR-ji-tate): to bring up food from the stomach; to vomit

**waterproof** (WAW-tur-proof): able to get wet without getting soaked; protected from water

**webbed** (webd): having toes that are connected by skin, making it easier to swim

**wild** (wilde): natural places where no people live

# Thinking Questions

1. What are baby penguins called?
2. Name three body parts that baby penguins have.
3. What is a group of penguins called?
4. How do baby penguins eat?
5. What can penguins do once their feathers grow in?

# Index



# About the Author

**Madison Parker** spent her childhood in the city of Chicago, Illinois. A farm girl at heart, today she lives in Wisconsin with her husband and four children on a small farm with cows, goats, chickens, and two miniature horses named Harley and David. Her favorite dessert is vanilla frozen custard with rainbow sprinkles, even in the winter.